WORLDVIEW GUIDE

TREASURE ISLAND

Douglas Wilson

canonpress
Moscow, Idaho

Published by Canon Press
P.O. Box 8729, Moscow, Idaho 83843
800.488.2034 | www.canonpress.com

Treasure Island, *Worldview Guide for Treasure Island*
Copyright ©2019 by Douglas Wilson.
Cited page numbers come from the Canon Classics edition of the book (2017),
www.canonpress.com/books/canon-classics.

Cover design by James Engerbretson
Cover illustration by Forrest Dickison
Interior design by Valerie Anne Bost and James Engerbretson

Printed in the United States of America.

All Scripture Quotations taken from King James Version.

Wilson, Douglas, 1953- author.
Treasure Island worldview guide / Douglas Wilson.
Moscow, Idaho : Canon Press, [2019]
LCCN 2019011350 | ISBN 1591282578 (paperback : alk. paper)
LCSH: Stevenson, Robert Louis, 1850-1894. Treasure Island.
Classification: LCC PR5486 .W55 2019 | DDC 823/.8--dc23
LC record available at https://lccn.loc.gov/2019011350

A free end-of-book test and answer key are available for download at
www.canonpress.com/ClassicsQuizzes

19 20 21 22 23 24 9 8 7 6 5 4 3

CONTENTS

INTRODUCTION

Mark Twain once defined a classic as a book that everyone wants to have read, but nobody wants to read. By that cute definition, *Treasure Island* is not a classic at all. It is a book that is preeminently readable, and not only so, but it is readable by a demographic group not known for its prowess in the literary arts—viz. young boys. This is a book that is pitched almost perfectly to the imagination of a young boy, and on top of that it serves as a rollicking good story for everyone else. It is the archetypical pirate story.

THE WORLD AROUND

Treasure Island was first published in 1882. That was an eventful year, and since Stevenson's adventure novel was full of mayhem, we should begin with some of the real-time mayhem of 1882. That was the year that Queen Victoria was almost assassinated while boarding a train. And elsewhere in the world, somebody else who was a better shot successfully assassinated Morgan Earp in Tombstone, Arizona. Not only so, but the famous outlaw Jesse James was also killed in that year.

In the world of music, Tchaikovsky's 1812 Overture premiered in Moscow. Chuck Berry was not yet born. In the world of electricity, which was much younger than the world of music, Thomas Edison tested the first grand scale use of his new-fangled light bulb at Pearl Street Station in New York. Also in that same year, Edison created the first electric Christmas tree lights. This reduced the number of lit candles on Christmas trees, which was never a good idea in the first place.

Although we were still some distance from the World Series, the first national championship baseball series was played in 1882, pitting Chicago against Cincinnati. As a number of these events indicate, we were on the threshold of the modern world.

ABOUT THE AUTHOR

Robert Louis Stevenson was a Scottish writer of the Victorian era. He was born in Edinburgh in 1850, and died in Samoa in 1894. Known for many books, including *Kidnapped*, and *The Strange Case of Dr. Jekyll and Mr. Hyde*, and *A Child's Garden of Verses*, he is best known for *Treasure Island*, the prototypical story of pirate lore.

He came from a pious Presbyterian family, Scots style, and much of his life and writing is dominated by his tragic revolt against that heritage. Stevenson was the most difficult kind of infidel—he had been brought up in a sincere and conscientious Calvinism, which he rejected in favor of the loose living of the literary set. Like many Scots children of that era, he had the Shorter Catechism memorized. His father, Thomas Stevenson, took his son's infidelity hard, believing that it rendered his "whole life a failure." One of his son's literary friends was W.E. Henley, author of *Invictus* ("I am the master of my fate / I am the captain of my soul").

It would be easy to dismiss the elder Stevenson as an austere old-school Calvinist, one who drove his son away with a rod of hard rigor, that being the caricature of Calvinism. But the reverse is more likely the truth. Because of Stevenson's sickly childhood and life, and because of his father's genuine tenderness, it is likely that the younger Stevenson was simply spoiled. Thomas Stevenson was still supporting his son financially as late as 1885. "It is fortunate for me I have a father," the son wrote, "or I should long ago have died." [1]

All that said, however, the lines he wrote that are inscribed on his tombstone are altogether lovely:

> *Home is the sailor, home from the sea,*
> *And the hunter home from the hill.*

---

1. Iain Murry, *The Undercover Revolution* (Carlisle, PA: Banner of Truth, 2009), 24.

WHAT OTHER NOTABLES SAID

"[*Treasure Island*] was, first and last, a revolt against pessimism."

~ G.K. Chesterton, *Robert Louis Stevenson*[2]

"I can hardly think that healthy boys will ever let Stevenson's books of adventure die"

~ Arthur Conan Doyle[3]

"[Stevenson] was the spirit of boyhood tugging at the skirts of this old world of ours and compelling it to come back and play."

~ J.M. Barrie, "R.L.S"[4]

"The significant fact for me is the feeling we have as we close *King Solomon's Mines*, or, still more, *She*. 'If only …'

2. Vol. 18 of *The Collected Works of G.K. Chesterton* (San Francisco: Ignatius Press, 1991), 74.

3. *Through the Magic Door* (New York: Doubleday, Page, 1909), 271.

4. *Margaret Oglivy* (Charles Scribner, 1896), 146.

are the words that rise to our lips. If only we could have had this very same story told by a Stevenson, a Tolkien, or a William Golding."

~ C.S. Lewis[5]

"[Stevenson] seemed to pick the right word up on the point of his pen, like a man playing spillikins [pick-up sticks]."

~ G.K. Chesterton, *The Victorian Age in Literature*[6]

"No novel will serve its purpose so forcibly, or make its point so plainly, as a novel by Stevenson."

~ G.K. Chesterton, *Robert Louis Stevenson*[7]

"a writer called Mr. Robert Louis Stevenson who makes the most delicate inlay-work in black and white, and files out to the fraction of a hair."

~ Rudyard Kipling, original draft of *Black Jack*

"Of all the stories that I have ever read I place Stevenson's *Treasure Island* first."

~ Jack London, Letter, December 24, 1914

---

5. C. S. Lewis, "Review of Rider Haggard: His Life and Works by Morton Cohen," in *Image and Imagination* (New York: HarperOne, 2014), EPub Edition, 321.

6. G.K. Chesteron, *The Victorian Age in Literature* (London: Henry Holt and Co., 1913), 246.

7. *The Collected Works of G.K. Chesterton,* vol. 18, *Thomas Carlyle, Leo Tolstoy, Robert Louis Stevenson, Chaucer* (San Francisco: Ignatius Press, 1991), 144.

SETTING, CHARACTERS, AND PLOT SUMMARY

The story begins at an inn in the West Coast of England, though it eventually shifts to a distant island in the Caribbean in the 1750s. The protagonist is Jim Hawkins, a young man who has never been to the sea before.

Jim's father is dead, and he and his mother run the Admiral Benbow Inn. A permanent guest there is an old salt, an ex-pirate, named Billy Bones. As the story opens, Billy Bones receives the black spot from his old shipmates—that spot being a sign of judgment and rejection among the pirates.

When Billy Bones dies, as his creditors, Jim and his mother go through his old sea chest and there find a treasure map. Jim shows the map to a nearby gentleman named Squire Trelawney. They realize what they have in their possession—a map to the treasure horde of the old pirate Captain Flint—and so the squire organizes an expedition to find it.

Unfortunately, Trelawney is somewhat foolish, naïve, and talkative, and the ship he commissions winds up with a crew that is largely comprised of Flint's old pirate crew. There are some honest sailors in their midst, but by and large, the whole expedition is a bad business. The captain of the ship is Captain Smollet, who is one of the honest ones.

The principal villain is the ship's cook, Long John Silver, a larger than life character, the great "stand-out" character in the book. When Jim happens to overhear Silver plotting the inevitable pirate mutiny, he warns the good guys, and forewarned is forearmed.

When they come to the island, the two forces are divided. The good guys occupy a stockade on the island at first, but then the positions are reversed and the pirates hold the stockade.

An old pirate named Ben Gunn had been marooned on the island years before, and as it turns out *he* had discovered the treasure some time before, and removed it all to his cave.

When they leave the island with the treasure, they maroon the remaining pirates, although they do take Long John Silver with them. In a port of call on the way home, Silver slips away with some of the treasure, and disappears from the story forever. But not from our hearts.

WORLDVIEW ANALYSIS

Treasure Island is certainly a story of treasure (and greed and ambition), and on top of that it is a rollicking good swashbuckler, a true adventure story. But the central treasure "gained" in the book is that of Jim's courage and maturity. This is a coming-of-age story come in the form of an adventure story.

When the story opens, Jim is a timid boy. By the end of the book, he has outwitted pirates, killed Israel Hands, set his mother up financially for life, and made a truly courageous decision for the sake of keeping his word.

In addition to being a coming-of-age story, it is also a "quest" story. The quest is to recover Flint's treasure, and there are various obstacles or guardians in the way. These guardians include the pirates at the Admiral Benbow Inn, the machinations of Long John Silver, and the helpful "obstruction" of Ben Gunn.

When the book opens, Jim has lost his father, and in the course of him coming of age, he grows to the point where he does not need a surrogate father—although various fathers are "offered." Among the contenders would be Squire Trelawney, who is too foolish, Captain Smollett, who is too strait-laced, and then, at the other end of the spectrum, Long John Silver, who is preeminently likeable, but is also unfortunately a scoundrel. Apart from his wickedness, he would have been a great dad.

So, to recap, a boy finds a treasure map, and together with some trustworthy friends, goes in search of that treasure. Some pirates, whose treasure it was, find out about the expedition and insinuate themselves into the crew, in the hopes of getting their hands on the swag again. A rollicking good time is had by some of the characters, and certainly by the reader, and who but an astounding *dullard* would think of trying to write a "worldview guide" for something like this? The next thing you know, someone is going to put out worldview study questions for the *Tintin* comic book series.

Part of our problem is that we tend to think we are turning everything into a "subject." As a result of that, we think we are becoming increasingly studious and scholarly. What is actually happening is that the current is running the opposite direction. The entertainment imperative is creeping into everything. It used to be that to have an entertaining book like *Treasure Island* incorporated into the *curriculum* would have been scorned by schoolmasters from here to Timbukthree. In school you studied "the greats" and you entertained yourself with well-written popular literature on your own time, preferably under the covers and with a flashlight.

The nervousness of the older grammarians is certainly vulnerable to ridicule whenever we look at a book that was once "popular literature," but which has proven itself a classic over time. But our lax standards would be an easy target for these nervous grammarians and schoolmasters from two centuries ago were they to travel down to our time, discovering here that you can attend various universities to take courses in *Demystifying the Hipster* (Tufts), *The Sociology of Miley Cyrus: Race, Class, Gender, and Media* (Skidmore), and *Kanye Versus Everybody!* (Georgia State University). We are at the bottom of a slippery slope that perhaps began by studying *Pride and Prejudice* instead of *The Odyssey* in the original Greek.

C.S. Lewis represented the sentiment of this older perspective very well.

> There is an intrinsic absurdity in making current literature a subject of academic study, and the student who wants a tutor's assistance in reading the works of his own contemporaries might as well ask for a nurse's assistance in blowing his own nose. [8]

But be that as it may, here we are now, and *Treasure Island* is in your curriculum. Here we are now, and you are reading it. The fact that you are enjoying it thoroughly is simply a by-product, and that can't really be helped. Try to keep a solemn face on it, as this is part of your education.

---

8. C. S. Lewis, "Our English Syllabus," in *Image and Imagination* (New York: HarperOne, 2014), EPub Edition, 30.

This is a story of high adventure, and this book is one of the books that helped establish the era of piracy on the high seas as a fixed era in the Western imagination. We might as well try to understand why we like it so much.

As mentioned earlier, the story is a coming-of-age tale, and in addition to that is also a quest. The implication is that Jim Hawkins grows up into maturity and virtue on account of his *experience*. But experience can take a young man in many directions. Experience by itself is blind. Long John Silver had a lot of experience also. Experience of what? Experience it why? Experience is a boat in the slow river of life, but still experience is no rudder. In order to know how to navigate the river, you need to have a standard. A standard enables you to steer left here, and right there. A standard answers the question *why*. Someone who would steer needs to get a hand on a map somehow.

We have an illustration of this necessity in the very setup of the novel. The pirate Flint was notorious, and had hidden his treasure years before. But no one seriously thought of going out to look for it until they had a *map* to narrow things down a bit. Otherwise they would have launched out, as that singular interpretation of this story put it, in the *Muppets' Treasure Island*, onto "that big blue wet thing."

Jim certainly has a standard that he lives by, and it is not simple self-interest. Although his character is not fully developed as the story opens, he is obviously a *good* boy.

This comes out in various ways. When Jim first overhears the planned mutiny, there is never any question of what side he is on. He is with "the good guys." Informing them of the plotted mutiny goes without saying. For another example, Jim gave his word to Long John Silver that he would not run away, and even Dr. Livesey urges him to break his word. This Jim refuses to do, which is certainly noble. This episode in the book is genuinely revelatory. But, given the terms of the book, *why* is it noble?

Surely there is more to morality than simply avoiding that which is "simply not done." This would simply reduce morality to manners. And are the pirates those who are guilty of nothing more than a breach of etiquette? Jim gave his word to Long John Silver, and he endangers himself by keeping his word. This is obviously a code, but a code has to come from somewhere. The pirates have their own code, their own laws, and yet they are considered wicked. What is Jim implicitly appealing to when he chooses to live by this code?

If it is merely the code of England, and no transcendental reference beyond that, then Jim is simply following the code of the larger group. But *that* should make us think of another pirate, as Augustine records it, who once was captured and asked Alexander the Great why he was considered a pirate for doing to ships what Alexander would do to countries.

No, Jim had a *true* code, which meant that it was somehow larger than all of us. When the doctor wanted to talk with him, Long John Silver made Jim to "give his word of honour as a young gentleman" that he would not "slip his cable." This promise Jim readily gave, and so was allowed to go out and confer with the doctor. What Jim is facing is not only death, but also the prospect of torture. When he considers that, he quails. "what I fear is torture. If they come to torture me—" With that the doctor interrupts him, and urges him to break his word. "Jim I can't have this. Whip over, and we'll run for it."

Jim's reply—in the face of *torture*—is this: "Doctor," said I, "I passed my word."

The doctor still tries to persuade him, and Jim reminds him that he would not do the thing himself, and so he shouldn't ask Jim to do it. Silver just a moment before had praised Doctor Livesey "You're a good man and a true; I never seen a better man!" This testimony is exactly right, but the doctor buckled under this terrible pressure before Jim did.

One other thing is worth noting while we are here. Stevenson accomplishes something quite striking in his creation of Long John Silver. Every Christian knows that we are sinners, and that every noble protagonist in literature has a streak of cussedness in him somewhere. For noble characters to have flaws is something that actually goes without saying for us. But in Long John Silver Stevenson has created a genuinely wicked character with streaks of charm, wit, affection, and ... *kindness*? The relationship of good and evil in characters is complicated, not two-dimensional.

Stevenson's pirates really are bad, but what do we mean by *bad*? We have Long John Silver, whom we are (intermittently) tempted to sympathize with, and we have Ben Gunn, with whom we really do sympathize. But Ben Gunn—not that long before—was one of the pirates. Was it the mere passage of time by himself that turned him into a sympathetic figure? Was it the fact that he spent all that time alone, sitting on the beach, reflecting on his misdeeds? What fixed him?

The answer to all these questions lies in the culture that produced Stevenson, even though he was a prodigal son running away from that culture. G.K. Chesterton argues that *Treasure Island* tells us a lot about Stevenson himself. Stevenson's "true private life is to be sought not in Samoa but in Treasure Island; for where the treasure is there is the heart also."[9] Stevenson has a code, and he shares this code with Jim. It is a *defined* code, but we don't know exactly where it is defined.

We know that Stevenson had rejected the Calvinistic faith of his father, and was not living as a Christian. But there are many people—and Stevenson certainly among them—who find that the Christian faith is not all that easy to walk away from. A lot of it comes with you when you try to go. This is something that Chesterton pointed to quite plainly.

---

9. *Collected Works of G.K. Chesterton*, vol. 18, 48.

> There is really and seriously an influence of Scottish Puritanism upon Stevenson.... He remained to the day of his death in some ways particularly loyal to the Presbyterian tradition.[10]

Given how these things usually go, the thing Stevenson did not successfully do is reject the culture that birthed him root and branch. I mentioned the prodigal son a moment ago, and so let us use that image to expand our understanding of Stevenson's relationship to his upbringing.

When someone rebels against the code they were brought up in, they are usually just rebelling against a few high profile items. The rest of their cultural heritage they are good with, assuming that those things are just a function of being civilized, not being Christian. For example, in the current apostasy against Christian culture, the rebellion against Christian sexual ethics has been pronounced and obvious. Nobody rebels against the idea of people forming up in orderly lines all by themselves when they arrive at the post office. In other words, people assume that they can throw certain obvious Christian doctrines overboard—but they also tend to assume that anything they don't want to throw overboard must not be Christian. But that is not at all the case.

Another way of putting this is that if the Christian faith spent a millennium and a half profoundly shaping the customs and mores of Western culture, you cannot simply reject this or that artifact of it and think you have

10. *Collected Works of G.K. Chesterton*, vol. 18, 88–89.

dealt with the whole. This is like having an architect design your house, live in it for twenty-five years, and then think you have rejected the architect and all his ways by knocking over the mailbox out front. The rest of the house is still there, and you are still living in it.

There is a point when consistent unbelief comes to the place of nihilism and despair. There is a point in unbelief where the residents of the house decide to deny the architect by burning the house down—and it has to be admitted that in our day the culture of unbelief is a lot closer to *that* place than Stevenson was when he rejected Christianity. This is why people like Stevenson can reject this or that aspect of Christianity, and believe that they are rejecting the entirety of it. The apostasy is real because they do deny the architect, and they *did* drive over the mailbox.

So at the end of the day, Stevenson had an acute sense of fair play, and that code was a Christian one. Not surprisingly, Jim shares it. Like Stevenson, he does not appeal to Christ, or give glory to God. But whether or not Stevenson does, or Jim does, the reader still can.

QUOTABLES

1. "Fifteen men on the Dead Man's Chest Yo-ho-ho, and a bottle of rum! Drink and the devil had done for the rest Yo-ho-ho, and a bottle of rum!"

   ~ Pirate Song, Chapter 1

2. "If it comes to a swinging, swing all, say I."

   ~ Pirate, Chapter 2

3. "'For thirty years,' he said, 'I've sailed the seas and seen good and bad, better and worse, fair weather and foul, provisions running out, knives going, and what not. Well, now I tell you, I never seen good come o' goodness yet. Him as strikes first is my fancy; dead men don't bite; them's my views—amen, so be it.'"

   ~ Israel Hands, Chapter 26

4. "It was Silver's voice, and before I had heard a dozen words, I would not have shown myself for all the world. I lay there, trembling and listening, in the extreme of

fear and curiosity, for, in those dozen words, I un-
derstood that the lives of all the honest men aboard
depended on me alone."

~ Jim Hawkins, Chapter 10

5.   "'One more step, Mr. Hands,' said I, 'and I'll blow your
     brains out! Dead men don't bite, you know,' I added
     with a chuckle.'"

~ Jim Hawkins, Chapter 26

6.   "In the immediate nearness of the gold, all else had
     been forgotten ... and I could not doubt that he
     hoped to seize upon the treasure, find and board the
     Hispanola under cover of night, cut every honest
     throat about that island, and sail away as he had at first
     intended, laden with crimes and riches."

~ Jim Hawkins, Chapter 32

7.   "It was a master surgeon, him that ampytated me—out
     of college and all—Latin by the bucket, and what not;
     but he was hanged like a dog, and sun-dried like the
     rest, at Corso Castle."

~ Long John Silver, Chapter 11

21 SIGNIFICANT
QUESTIONS AND ANSWERS

1. Why do we like yarns and pirate stories?

> Not every story needs to be dark and artsy; stories
> with black hats and white hats are fine. Stories that
> have a pirate with a wooden leg are doubly fine.
> This story found in *Treasure Island* is authentic, and
> also exotic. There is shiny treasure, bright seas, pi-
> rate trappings, and what's not to like? We also enjoy
> the presentation of the ideal of manhood—man at
> sea is very much exploring and mastering nature,
> but not overpowering it.

2. Should we write worldview guides for *everything*?

> Well, actually, we shouldn't have to. But if we learn to
> think like Christians when it comes to great litera-
> ture, we should be able to navigate popular literature
> on our own.

3.   Why would older school teachers have objected to the
     study of a book like *Treasure Island* in school?

> It would have been assumed that literature by their
> contemporaries is something that students should
> be able to handle on their own. It would have been
> thought that great literature would be far more
> challenging, and the students would be in greater
> need of instruction and help. This would be because
> of language barriers, the challenges created by the
> passage of time, and by the aesthetic challenges that
> are involved.
>
> For example, a modern high school student would
> need to have a great deal explained to him if he
> were to read and enjoy Homer's *Odyssey*. But he
> needs a lot of background information—what the
> Trojan War was about, how Greek poetry worked,
> what translations can and cannot do, and so on. He
> doesn't have the same problem when he picks up
> a book written for his age group, with a copyright
> from last year.

4.   What is great literature?

> Great literature is not just serious-themed or some-
> thing that is interesting to talk about, but includes
> challenging stories that are difficult and take time
> to read and understand and which should change
> us. A certain high level of artistry is called for, and
> if the book has survived the test of time, we know
> that many people have thought that it achieved that

high level of artistry. Still, the corn dogs of literature are not to be despised. Especially when they
are good corn dogs.

5. What genres influence *Treasure Island*? The navy yarn?
    The desert island story?

    This story is similar to *Robinson Crusoe*—it occurs
    in roughly the same era and is a story of the sea
    when exploring the seas was still relatively new. It is
    also similar to later stories like those about Horatio
    Hornblower, the era when the British Navy that
    ruled the world. This is the era of the swashbuckler.

6. What kind of story is *Treasure Island*? How is *Treasure
    Island* a Bildungsroman? Why does Jim's father die at
    the beginning of the novel?

    A Bildungsroman is a "coming of age story," which
    is what Treasure Island most certainly is. It is also a
    quest story. So this is a coming of age story, mean-
    ing that it occurs at a momentous and formative
    time in the protagonist's life. It is a story about
    when the protagonist discovers the world, and then
    grows up into it. Jim's father dies right at the begin-
    ning of the novel, and right around the same time
    that Billy Bones dies. And so Jim is truly orphaned;
    he is truly on his own. In the course of the story Jim
    jumps off the boat, makes his own way, meets Ben
    Gunn, fights in battle, takes the ship from Israel
    Hands, and survives the treasure hunt. By the end
    of the story, we see that he has become a man.

7.   What is it that causes Jim Hawkins to grow and
     mature?

> The initial answer is that he has matured because of
> experience. It is an adventure story, and so it is not
> surprising that he has lots of adventures. But ma-
> turity is not something that automatically happens
> to people who have adventures. Adventures destroy
> some people.

8.   So why is this answer of experience an inadequate one?

> It is inadequate because every character has expe-
> rience. All the pirates were experienced. Ben Gunn
> was experienced. But we all—and Jim Hawkins—
> need a standard that will help us as we navigate
> our experiences. Experience is like a test, and not
> everyone passes every test.

9.   What is a standard like? Does Jim have a standard or a
     code that he lives by?

> A standard is like a map that tells you where you
> need to go, or what you need to do.

> Jim certainly does have a standard, and it is a noble
> one. For example, Jim is unwilling to break his
> promise to a pirate, even though refusing to break
> that promise might result in him being tortured by
> the other pirates.

10. Would Dr. Livesey have broken his word in order to save his own life?

> No, he would not have done so. This standard or code is one that Dr. Livesey and Jim obviously share. Jim knows that Dr. Livesey would do the same thing he is doing if their positions were reversed. But Dr. Livesey feels responsible for Jim's safety, and so he wanted to take onto his own shoulders the burden of Jim breaking his word. It wouldn't be as bad if he did that, because he wouldn't be doing it to save his own skin, but rather to save the life of another.

11. What did the pirate ask Alexander the Great?

> He asked him why he was considered a pirate for doing to ships what Alexander did to countries, and yet Alexander was styled a great emperor. This is actually a reasonable question, although Alexander might not have thought so. The reason this is worth reflecting on is because Jim's standard has to be rooted in something greater than the code of the English. Why should the code of the English outrank the code of the pirates? In other words, in order to be of any use at all, the standard or code has to be anchored outside our world completely.

12. Why was Jim's code a true code, honestly held?

> Because it had authority outside of Jim's circum-stances and experience. He held to it even though doing so might cost him a great deal.

13. Why is Long John Silver a peculiar villain?

> He is genuinely wicked, and yet there are a number
> of endearing traits about him, including things like
> affection and kindness. He is very wicked, but he
> is also very human. You get the feeling, by the end
> of the book, that if Silver came to you in order to
> plead for something, you might have trouble turn-
> ing him down. Even though you knew that he was
> probably lying to you.

14. Why are there are no women in the story?

> We shouldn't overthink things like this. They were
> out at sea, and women were not very common out
> there. In addition, the presence of women would
> have the additional effect of turning the story into
> another kind of story completely. This is a romance
> that doesn't need to turn into the other kind of
> romance. On top of everything else, the book was
> written for boys, and therefore contains all the
> elements that boys would find attractive. It does not
> need to contain the elements that they do not (yet)
> find attractive.

15. What do the characters all contribute to the story?

> Smollett is honest but too strict. On the opposite
> end, Squire Trelawney too easygoing—after all, he
> winds up hiring a crew of pirates. And while we
> have a host of pirates, there are different kinds of
> pirates. Jim has to learn to see through Silver, he

has to negotiate with Israel Hands, and he has to use Ben Gunn's greed.

16. Did Stevenson successfully escape his conservative Christian upbringing? What is his rejection of Christianity compared to in the essay? What is rejected?

> No, he did not escape it. Rejecting the faith is like rejecting the authority of an architect while still living in a house that the architect designed. Only the obvious traits of the faith are rejected—the formal authority of the faith, the deity of Christ, or Christian sexual ethics. But though you might erase the architect's name from the blueprints, the house is still there. And you are still living in it.

17. How do unbelievers account for why they keep certain aspects of their Christian heritage?

> They assume that such things are just the fruit of generic civilization. If I throw overboard certain Christian doctrines, it is easy to believe that anything I like and don't want to throw over must not be part of the Christian heritage. But that does not follow. If you have seen everybody do certain things your whole life, like stand in line at the post office in an orderly manner, and everybody does this, believer and unbeliever alike, it is easy to assume that belief and unbelief have nothing to do with little civilizational traits, like standing in line. But all it should take is one visit to a country where nobody

waits in line. Another example, one that is a bit
more important, would be monogamy. Many people
in our culture today just assume that monogamy
is normal for civilized people—but it took many
centuries for the Christian faith to get this custom
adopted by our culture.

18. So is there a point where unbelief has to reject "the
whole house?"

> Yes, that happens in the late stages of apostasy. But
> early on it is easy for the prodigal son to use mon-
> ey and resources he got from his father without
> giving any real credit to his father. In Stevenson's
> case, he was a prodigal who was not that far out
> from his father's house. He was running away
> from home, but had only made it down to the end
> of the driveway. That meant that the culture of
> unbelief appeared to have a lot more going for it
> than it actually did. Nobility was still prized, and
> Jim exhibits it in a marvelous way. But if there is
> no God, then what is so bad about double-cross-
> ing a pirate?

19. What does it look like in the late stages of unbelief?

> It looks like burning the house down, which is far
> more than knocking the mailbox down out in front
> of the house. The end result of unbelief is always
> going to be some form of nihilism, the corrosive
> of complete skepticism. But the problem with this
> corrosive is that it eats up every container you try

to keep it in. In other words, it does not just eat up the Christian faith, but also reason, experience, tradition, and our own sense of self. If I have to doubt everything, then that means I have to doubt that I am able to doubt.

20. So was Stevenson's code a Christian one?

Yes, far more than he knew.

21. Does this wreck the book for us?

No. Although he didn't acknowledge it, we certainly can.

FURTHER DISCUSSION AND REVIEW

Master what you have read by reviewing and integrating the different elements of this classic.

SETTING AND CHARACTERS
Be able to compare and contrast the personalities (including strengths, weaknesses, and mannerisms) of each character. Which characters change over the course of the novel? Which do not?

PLOT
Be able to describe the beginning, middle, and end of the book along with specific details that move the plot forward and make it compelling.

CONFLICT
Go through the character list and describe the tension between any and all main characters. Then, think about

whether any characters have internal conflict (in their own minds). Is there any overt conflict (fighting), or conflict with impersonal forces?

THEME STATEMENTS

Be able to describe what this classic is telling us about the world. Is the message true? What truth can we take from the plot, characters, conflict, and themes (even if the author didn't believe that truth)? Do any objects take on added meaning because of repetition or their place in the story (i.e., do any objects become symbols)? How does the author use perspective, tone, and irony to tell the truth?

- Keep your word, deal honesty, and fight pirates.
- A fool and his money are soon parted.
- Using the standard classification for characters, which characters in this book are "round" and which are "flat?" Which characters do you feel like you know by the end of the book, and which characters not? Does a character need to have divided sympathies in order to be "round?" Is complexity a part of it? Is ethical complexity part of it? Spend some time discussing the complexity of a character like Long John Silver, and compare it to the simplicity of a character like Captain Smollett.

A NOTE FROM THE PUBLISHER:
TAKING THE CLASSICS QUIZ

Once you have finished the worldview guide, you can prepare for the end-of-book test. Each test will consist of a short-answer section on the book itself and the author, a short-answer section on plot and the narrative, and a long-answer essay section on worldview, conflict, and themes.

Each quiz, along with other helps, can be downloaded for free at www.canonpress.com/ClassicsQuizzes. If you have any questions about the quiz or its answers or the Worldview Guides in general, you can contact Canon Press at service@canonpress.com or 208.892.8074.

ABOUT THE AUTHOR

Douglas Wilson has been a pastor of Christ Church in Moscow, Idaho for forty years. He has started both a K-12 Christian school and an accredited Christian college and has written more than fifty books. He and his wife Nancy have three children, all of whom have witten books of their own, and he is the grandfather to a bunch of grandchildren.